Editor
Eric Migliaccio

Managing Editor
Ina Massler Levin, M.A.

Editor-in-Chief
Sharon Coan, M.S. Ed.

Cover Artist
Barb Lorseyedi

Art Manager
Kevin Barnes

Imaging
James Edward Grace

Product Manager
Phil Garcia

Publisher
Mary D. Smith, M.S. Ed.

Practice Makes Perfect

Main Idea

GRADE 5

Includes practice for Standardized Tests

Author

Debra J. Housel, M.S. Ed.

Teacher Created Resources

Teacher Created Resources, Inc.
6421 Industry Way
Westminster, CA 92683
www.teachercreated.com
ISBN-0-7439-8645-8
©2004 Teacher Created Resources, Inc.
Reprinted, 2005
Made in U.S.A.

Table of Contents

Introduction

The old adage "practice makes perfect" can apply to your child and his or her education. The more practice and exposure your child has with concepts being taught in school, the more success he or she is likely to find. For many parents, knowing how to help their children may be frustrating because the resources may not be readily available. As a parent, it is also hard to know where to focus your efforts so that the extra practice your child receives at home supports what he or she is learning in school.

A child's ability to understand what he or she reads depends largely upon the ability to locate the main idea of a passage and identify the details that support it. *Practice Makes Perfect: Main Idea* covers identifying the main idea and supporting details in both fiction and nonfiction text. To allow for the greatest variety of practice, the passages are not complete stories. The exercises included in this book meet or reinforce educational standards and objectives similar to the ones required by your state and school district for fifth-graders:

- ☞ The student will identify the main idea in fiction and nonfiction text.

- ☞ The student will locate supporting details in fiction and nonfiction text.

- ☞ The student will identify topic sentences in paragraphs.

- ☞ The student will choose the best title for a passage.

- ☞ The student will summarize the main idea of a passage.

Introduction *(cont.)*

How to Make the Most of This Book

☞ Set aside a specific place in your home to work on this book. Keep the necessary materials on hand.

☞ Determine a specific time of day to work on these practice pages to establish consistency. Look for times in your day or week that are conducive to practicing skills.

☞ Keep all practice sessions with your child positive and constructive. If your child becomes frustrated or tense, set aside the book and look for another time to practice. Do not force your child to perform or use this book as a punishment.

☞ Allow the child to use whatever writing instrument he or she prefers.

☞ Review and praise the work your child has done.

Things to Remember About the Main Idea in Nonfiction

Make certain that your child understands the way that authors typically present ideas in nonfiction materials. Nonfiction writers use four different paragraph structures. For each type, the main idea is italicized:

Paragraph Structure #1

Usually the main idea is directly stated as the first sentence of a paragraph. The rest of the paragraph provides the supporting details:

> *Clara Barton, known as America's first nurse, was a brave and devoted humanitarian.* While caring for others, she was shot at, got frostbitten fingers, had severe laryngitis twice, burned her hands, and almost lost her eyesight. Yet she continued to care for the sick and injured until she died at the age of 91.

Paragraph Structure #2

Once in a while the main idea may appear in the center of the paragraph, surrounded on both sides by details:

> The coral have created a reef where more than 200 kinds of birds and about 1,500 types of fish live. *In fact, Australia's Great Barrier Reef provides a home for a great variety of interesting animals.* These include sea turtles, giant clams, crabs, and crown-of-thorns starfish.

Paragraph Structure #3

Often the main idea comes at the end of the paragraph as a summary of the details that came before:

> Each year Antarctica spends six months in darkness, from mid March to mid September. The continent is covered year-round by ice, which causes sunlight to reflect off its surface. It never really warms up. The coldest temperature ever recorded on Earth was in Antarctica. *Antarctica has one of the harshest environments in the world.*

Things to Remember About the Main Idea in Nonfiction *(cont.)*

Paragraph Structure #4

Sometimes the main idea is not directly stated and must be inferred from the details given in the paragraph. This paragraph structure is the most challenging for children:

> The biggest sea horse ever found was over a foot long. Large sea
> horses live along the coasts of New Zealand, Australia, and California.
> Smaller sea horses live off the coast of Florida, in the Caribbean
> Sea, and in the Gulf of Mexico. The smallest adult sea horse ever
> found was only one half-inch long!

In this example, the implied main idea is that sea horses' sizes vary based on where they live. When the main idea isn't stated, the student must pull together the details to ascertain the key idea. A good way to do this is to think about the "reporter questions": who, (did) what, when, where, why, and how. The passage may present the answers in any order; however, not all of the questions can always be answered.

Things to Remember About the Main Idea in Fiction

☞ Unlike nonfiction text, literature rarely has paragraphs with topic sentences and supporting details. Often in fictional text the main idea is never directly stated anywhere in the passage. This can present a challenging task for your young student. One of the best ways for a student to ascertain the main idea in fiction is to "form a movie" in his or her mind. This changing visualization will help the child to figure out the key idea.

☞ Just as they do in nonfiction, the answers to the questions *who, did what, when, where, why,* and *how* lead a reader to the details in fiction. A compilation of the details can also be helpful in identifying the main idea. Even so, without a topic sentence, stating the main idea requires paraphrasing, which is a higher-level thinking skill.

☞ In literature, the main idea is often embedded in emotions—the emotions of the characters and the emotions of the reader. Well-written fiction makes the reader feel as if he or she is "there" and actually experiencing the events in the story. Therefore, encourage your student to notice the emotions of the characters. Ask leading questions such as, "How would you feel if you were [character's name]? Why? Do you think [character's name] feels like you do? Why?"

The main idea is what a paragraph or passage is about overall. The main idea is frequently stated in a sentence and then supported by details within the paragraph.

Passage 1

People have always had ideas they wanted to share with others. Early people drew pictures on cave walls to show how to hunt deer and woolly mammoths. Eventually people around the world started to write. Each group came up with a different way. The Egyptians used hieroglyphs, with each picture standing for a sound. People in parts of Asia made marks in clay called cuneiforms. The Chinese and Japanese people created a separate symbol for each word. They continue to use this system today.

What is the main idea?

ⓐ The Chinese and Japanese people designed a symbol for each of their words.

ⓑ People have always tried to share ideas with others.

ⓒ Cave people made pictures to show others how to hunt.

ⓓ Eventually people around the world started to write.

Passage 2

"Look over there!" one of the greedy dragons pointed. "We didn't notice that door before. I bet there's more gold behind it."

Both of them rushed to the door, rudely shoving each other in an attempt to be the first to open it and claim the spoils. In their haste, they tore the door off its hinges. Immediately stinging insects and animals burst forth. Scorpions and snakes dug their fangs into the dragons' scaly tails, while hornets and bees buzzed about their heads. A noisy mob of mosquitoes flew right into the dragons' faces.

Filled with terror, the dragons fled from the cottage. They rushed blindly down the hill, tripping over stones and stumbling into bushes. Reaching the pond, they ducked under the water to escape from their attackers. But it was no use, for a dragon cannot hold its breath any longer than a human can. Every time they lifted their heads to get a gulp of air, the poisonous horde renewed its assault.

What is the main idea?

ⓐ The greedy dragons are seeking gold.

ⓑ The dragons damage a door in their quest for gold.

ⓒ The dragons try to escape from stinging bugs and animals.

ⓓ The dragons enjoy hiding in a pond.

Passage 3

In space, there is very little gravity. Even so, any really large thing will still pull smaller things toward it. The bigger something is, the stronger its gravity. Jupiter is so huge that all of the other planets could fit inside of it! Jupiter's gravity pulls on rocks floating in space and as they move closer, they start circling the planet. They're held in place by Jupiter's gravity. This is why Jupiter has 60 moons.

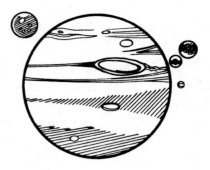

What is the main idea?

(a) Jupiter is so large that it could hold all of the other planets together.

(b) In space, there's very little gravity.

(c) Jupiter has strong gravity.

(d) Jupiter has 60 moons.

Passage 4

For as long as the oldest chipmunk in Squeaker's family could remember, the oak tree had dropped lots of acorns. The chipmunks picked them up and stored them in their burrows beneath its roots or under nearby bushes. The tree had sustained them so well that there had never been a need to look elsewhere for food.

But something had gone wrong this summer. No leaves had ever come out, leaving the normally cool, shady ground beneath its branches hot, dry, and sunny. Now it was autumn and not a single acorn lay on the ground. The oak tree didn't drop even one. When Papa went up to explore the branches, he found none there. He did see another big oak tree, but it stood on the other side of the road.

One of Squeaker's relatives had tried to go across the road long ago. She had never returned. No chipmunks had ever tried again.

What is the main idea?

(a) The chipmunks enjoy living beneath an oak tree.

(b) Squeaker's relative never returned after crossing the great gray danger.

(c) Something is wrong with the oak tree.

(d) The chipmunks' acorn supply is no longer available.

Passage 5

Many people are surprised when they learn that temperature determines whether a baby turtle becomes a male or female. First a mother turtle chooses a sandy, sunny spot near a pond. She digs an L-shaped hole and fills it with eggs. Males hatch from the eggs in the warmest part of the nest. The eggs in the cooler area will be females. Some years, if the summer has a very long hot or cold spell, the turtles will be all the same sex.

What is the main idea?

ⓐ The nest temperature determines whether a baby turtle is a female or male.

ⓑ If a summer is especially hot, all turtle babies are male.

ⓒ During cool summers most turtle babies are females.

ⓓ A mother turtle digs a hole and fills it with eggs.

Passage 6

Although most people think Christopher Columbus discovered America, Leif Ericsson was probably the first European to visit the New World. Leif was a sailor. He left his home in Norway to go to Greenland. When he found Greenland covered with ice, he wondered if there might be better land further west. He set sail around 1000 A.D.

He landed in Canada. He named it Vinland. Then he returned to tell others about the place. The next year men and women set off to build homes in the new land. However, the Native Americans did not want the people there. They wrecked their villages many times. Around 1005 A.D. the Norse people gave up.

The Norse people had oral legends about what happened. But no one was sure if the stories were true. Now a Norse spindle has been dug up in Newfoundland. A woman used it to spin wool into yarn 1,000 years ago. Although many people used spindles, only the Norse people used this kind. This simple tool proves that they were in America long before Columbus set sail.

What is the main idea?

ⓐ A Norse spindle has been dug up in Newfoundland.

ⓑ Canada was originally called Vinland by Leif Ericsson.

ⓒ The Native Americans disliked the Norse people.

ⓓ Evidence shows that the Norse people were in America almost 500 years before Columbus.

Passage 7

Global warming is a form of air pollution. It is caused by too much carbon dioxide in the atmosphere. Although carbon dioxide is a natural element, a great deal of it is released daily by engines, factories, and homes. Over time Earth's atmosphere has absorbed too much. The result has been rising temperatures and changes in the amounts of rainfall in different areas. These changes can cause problems for plants and animals. If they cannot adapt quickly, they die.

People want to pass laws to stop vehicles and factories from dumping so much carbon dioxide into the air. They hope to stop global warming.

What is the main idea?

(a) People want to stop global warming.

(b) If plants and animals cannot adapt quickly, they will die.

(c) Too much carbon dioxide in the air results in global warming, causing problems for livings things.

(d) Carbon dioxide is released into the atmosphere by engines, factories, and homes.

Passage 8

That afternoon as the two friends walked on the path through the woods, a large bear came out of the forest. The bear stood on the path directly in front of them and growled. Neither man had a weapon, and both were scared. Immediately Neil raced to a nearby tree and climbed up its branches.

Rob knew that he had no chance of defending himself against such a big bear. He had heard that bears wouldn't attack a dead body, so he threw himself on the ground and pretended to be dead. He closed his eyes and held his breath and hoped that the huge bear would leave him alone. The bear grunted in Rob's ear, sniffed and nuzzled around his nose and mouth, and pawed at his backpack. After doing this, the bear lumbered into the trees, heading away from the men.

What is the main idea?

(a) When two men meet a bear, one climbs a tree and the other plays dead.

(b) Rob must play dead when a bear approaches him.

(c) Neil climbs a tree to escape from a bear.

(d) Two friends work together to fend off a bear.

Passage 9

People must park their cars while they work or do business in a city. Yet there is rarely enough parking space. The Toronto Parking Authority decided to do something about this problem by parking cars in layers. In 1956 it built the first North American parking ramp in Canada.

Today parking ramps provide necessary parking space in a city. They hold hundreds of vehicles. Sometimes a parking garage is like many parking lots stacked on top of each other. Other times underground ramps are built in layers beneath tall buildings.

As a driver enters a parking garage, she takes a ticket. She drives on the ramp until she sees an open spot. She parks her car and goes about her business. When she returns, she drives to a booth at street level. She gives the ticket to a person in a booth. The ticket tells how much money she owes. After paying, the driver leaves the garage.

What is the main idea?

ⓐ People must pay to park in parking garages.

ⓑ Parking ramps provide necessary parking space in a city.

ⓒ The Toronto Parking Authority built the first North American parking ramp in 1956.

ⓓ People need to park their cars in cities.

Passage 10

Television shows and movies often make a cowboy's life look interesting and fun. In truth, a cowboy's life was tough. Cowboys rounded up cattle into herds of about 5,000 steers. After the cattle ate all of the grass in one area, they had to go to a new place. So the cowboys moved the herds over the hot, dusty prairie. They tried to stay away from hills and woods to avoid attacks by cattle thieves. If a cowboy got sick or injured, it could be several days' ride to reach medical help.

A chuck wagon carried all of their food, water, medicine, bedding, tents, and tools. The men usually had enough bread, beef, and beans to eat, but it was the same food day after day. The meat got so old that it was served hot and spicy to hide its taste. The luckiest cowboys created occasional pieces of dried fruit.

What is the main idea?

ⓐ Being a cowboy was a hard job.

ⓑ Cattle thieves often attacked cowboys.

ⓒ The luckiest cowboys got dried fruit to eat.

ⓓ A chuck wagon carried supplies for the cowboys.

You can picture the main idea as a flag flying at the top of a pole. The flag is what you notice first. It's what's most important, just like the main idea. The flagpole holds up the flag, just as the details hold up, or support, the main idea.

Details . . .

☞ **provide more facts about the main idea.**

☞ **offer reasons.**

☞ **give examples.**

Passage 1

The explorers held their torches high as they cautiously moved forward. No sooner had they stepped inside the tunnel than a great monster leaped from the shadows and blocked their way. The ugly beast had purple eyes. Above them a horn rose from the center of its forehead. Its bright orange skin showed beneath a thin layer of coarse, black hair. As it reached its claws toward the terrified group, it snarled menacingly, revealing a mouthful of sharp teeth.

The main idea is:

(a) The explorers discover a secret tunnel.

(b) A frightening monster stands before the explorers.

(c) An evil monster threatens to eat the explorers.

(d) The frightened explorers need to use torches inside a dark tunnel.

The main idea is supported by these six details:

1. _____

2. _____

3. _____

4. _____

5. _____

6. _____

Passage 2

When people see American symbols, they think of the U.S.A. America's oldest symbol is the Liberty Bell. It rang on July 4, 1776, when Americans first said that they were free from British rule.

The American flag is another symbol. It has one star for each state. It has a stripe for each of the first 13 states. The red stripes stand for bravery, and the white stripes stand for truth.

Congress chose the American bald eagle as the national bird in 1782. The American bald eagle lives only in North America. These birds symbolize strength, beauty, and long life.

The main idea is:

ⓐ America has symbols.

ⓑ The Liberty Bell is America's oldest symbol.

ⓒ The bald eagle was chosen as America's national bird because of its strength, beauty, and long life.

ⓓ The stripes on the American flag stand for bravery and truth.

The main idea is supported by these three details:

1. _____

2. _____

3. _____

Passage 3

People have damaged the Amazon rain forest. They have removed soil in search of precious metals. The dirt left behind is not suitable for growing anything. Millions of trees get cut down every year for furniture. With fewer trees, more soil washes away. Dams built to stop floods and make electrical power have backed up rivers. Blocking a river creates a lake that leaves everything underwater for miles behind the dam. All of these actions have left the world's largest rain forest in danger.

The main idea is:

ⓐ The world's largest rain forest is in the Amazon River Basin.

ⓑ Dams leave everything behind them underwater for miles.

ⓒ In the Amazon rain forest, trees are being cut down.

ⓓ People have done things that have hurt the Amazon rain forest.

The main idea is supported by these three details:

1. _____

2. _____

3. _____

Passage 4

Becky loved Grandma's home. It was cozy and welcoming, and she felt safe there. Inside the small, two-story house, heavy red velvet drapes hung at the front windows. A collection of china figurines shared the mantel with photos of grandchildren. Everything was clean and tidy. Sunlight streamed through the kitchen windows, nurturing flowering plants. Best of all, the air always had some delicious baking smell, such as oatmeal cookies or cherry pie.

The main idea is:

(a) Grandma's home is clean and tidy.

(b) Grandma is always baking something delicious.

(c) Becky loved Grandma's home.

(d) Becky visits her Grandma each day.

The main idea is supported by these four details:

1. _____   3. _____

2. _____   4. _____

Passage 5

The Native Americans called the Iroquois had a well-established nation. Several families, all related through the mother, lived in bark-covered long houses. They hunted with bows and arrows for deer, fish, turkeys, and other wild animals. They also grew squash, corn, beans, and berries. All food was shared among the members of the tribe so that everyone had enough to eat. When they were sick, their medicine men used herbal cures to make them well.

Women had an important role. They assigned and removed men from their tribe's government. Five Iroquois tribes joined to form the Iroquois League. They agreed that the five tribes would not fight with each other. They also agreed to help defend each other from outside attacks. Eventually a sixth tribe joined them.

The main idea is:

(a) Women played an important role in the Iroquois nation.

(b) Five Iroquois tribes joined to form the Iroquois League.

(c) The Iroquois used advanced herbal medicine to keep its tribe healthy.

(d) The Iroquois had a well-established nation.

The main idea is supported by these five details:

1. _____   4. _____

2. _____   5. _____

3. _____

Passage 6

Bright Lightning crept out of the bushes cautiously. Her eyes darted about, searching for the wolf, but it had disappeared. Yet in the clearing she was shocked to see a man, whose strength and magnificence was beyond that of any she had ever seen before. He wore a band of eagle feathers in his long, black hair, and his legs were clad in deerskin. He had a broad chest and muscular arms. Although he towered over her like a sturdy oak tree, his smile was kind. Bright Lightning knew that this man must be a great warrior or a chieftain. She stared at him in awe.

The main idea is:

ⓐ Bright Lightning is searching for a wolf.

ⓑ A strong, magnificent man asks Bright Lightning to marry him.

ⓒ Bright Lightning sees a magnificent man whom she believes is a chieftain or warrior.

ⓓ A strong, magnificent man chased Bright Lightning into the bushes.

The main idea is supported by these seven details:

1. _____   4. _____   7. _____

2. _____   5. _____

3. _____   6. _____

Passage 7

If the U.S.A. changed to the metric system, it would mean that Americans would have the same measuring system as the rest of the world. This could make trading with other countries simpler. It would increase the use of decimals and reduce the use of fractions. Since calculators use decimals and many people dislike fractions, that's a good thing. People in science and medicine already use metric measurements.

However, it would cost a lot to change all the current measurements in stores, factories, offices, and schools. And teaching everyone a new system could be hard and take a lot of time. Americans have always balked at the idea of learning the metric system. The adults say that they'd have trouble getting used to the new measurements. For example, 32°F is freezing, while 32°C is a very hot day.

The main idea is:

ⓐ There are both benefits and problems if the U.S. changes to the metric system.

ⓑ American adults would probably have difficulty getting used to metric measurements.

ⓒ The U.S.A. should switch to the metric system.

ⓓ The U.S.A. should not change to the metric system.

The main idea is supported by these six details:

1. _____   3. _____   5. _____

2. _____   4. _____   6. _____

Passage 8

America changed due to the swift movement of many people to the West. People made roads, built homes, and created new towns in a matter of months. This caused problems for the Native Americans. They did not want the settlers to come West. They wanted to go on with their way of life, following buffalo herds for food. The new roads went right through the areas where Native Americans lived and hunted. The settlers didn't want other people on their land. The Native Americans couldn't understand this. They did not believe that a person could own land. Unfortunately, the two groups usually did not work things out peacefully.

The main idea is:

ⓐ The settlers and Native Americans rarely worked out their disputes peacefully.

ⓑ The movement of people to the West disrupted the Native Americans' way of life.

ⓒ New roads went right through the areas where Native Americans lived and hunted.

ⓓ Native Americans did not believe that a person could own land.

The main idea is supported by these five details:

1. _____   4. _____

2. _____   5. _____

3. _____

Passage 9

Without plants there would be no life on Earth. They begin every food chain by supplying food for animals. Plants also keep the soil in its place and give off the oxygen that humans and most animals need to breathe. We also depend on plants for food, medicines, building materials, and cloth (such as cotton and linen). People called botanists study plants. They have already found more than half a million different kinds of plants. They realize there are still many more to discover.

The main idea is:

ⓐ Plants are essential for both animals and humans.

ⓑ There are still more plants to be discovered.

ⓒ Botanists have already found more than half a million different kinds of plants.

ⓓ People called botanists study plants.

The main idea is supported by these six details:

1. _____   4. _____

2. _____   5. _____

3. _____   6. _____

You can find the main idea and supporting details by looking for the answers to these questions:

☞ who or what   ☞ where

☞ did what   ☞ why

☞ when   ☞ how

Passage 1

She didn't need a second invitation, for her stomach grumbled with hunger. Claudia entered the home and put the sack with the leprechaun in it near her feet under the table. The farmer's wife set a plate filled with macaroni and cheese before each of them. However, Claudia did not intend to eat mere macaroni and cheese. She pressed her foot against the sack. The leprechaun squealed rather loudly.

"Sh!" said Claudia, but at the same time, pressed her foot on it again so that it squealed even louder.

"What have you got in your sack?" asked the farmer's wife.

"Oh, that's just my leprechaun," said Claudia. "He says there's no need for us to eat this macaroni and cheese. If you'll just look in your oven, he's conjured up a whole feast of roast chicken, mashed potatoes, and cherry pie." Of course Claudia knew that the wife had hidden this food in the oven, for she had seen her do so through the window.

The farmer jumped up and opened the oven door. He cried out in astonishment. "Why, there's a beautiful meal in here! It's fresh and hot, too!" Immediately the farmer began to plot how he could get the leprechaun away from Claudia.

Find in the passage the answers to these questions.

Who or What?: _____

Did What?: _____ tricked the farmer _____

When?: _____

Where?: _____

Why?: _____

How?: _____

Passage 2

Eight hundred years ago Native Americans, called the Anasazi, lived in the American Southwest. Their land was very dry, yet they grew crops. They dug ditches that provided water to their plants. They built their villages by carving out the clay in the sides of cliffs. Their homes were so well made that many of them still stand today.

No one knows what became of the Anasazi. They just disappeared about 600 years ago. Their villages show no signs of a war. They left no graves to indicate a wave of serious illness. We may never know what happened to them.

Find in the passage the answers to these questions.

Who or What?: _____

Did What?: _____

When?: _____

Where?: _____

Why?: _____no one knows_____

How?: _____

Passage 3

Have you ever had a chocolate chip cookie? Americans eat 7 billion of them each year. Few know that these cookies were invented accidentally in 1930. Ruth Wakefield ran the Toll House Inn in Massachusetts. She made food for the guests. One day as she mixed up a batch of chocolate cookies, she realized that she was out of baker's chocolate. She broke a chocolate bar into tiny pieces. She added the chocolate bits to the dough, hoping they would melt and spread throughout the cookies. When she took the cookie sheets from the oven, Ruth was upset to see that the chocolate chunks were still there. However, a guest wanted to try a cookie. He couldn't believe how good it tasted. Other guests ate the cookies and liked them, too. Ruth Wakefield had just invented chocolate chip cookies.

Find in the passage the answers to these questions.

Who or What?: _____

Did What?: _____

When?: _____

Where?: _____

Why?: _____

How?: _____the chocolate bits didn't melt into the cookies_____

Passage 4

The alligator waited patiently all day for some food to come along. He stayed absolutely still, alert for movement. He could stay completely under water for hours. If he got tired of doing that, he could keep most of his body underwater, with just his eyes at the surface. As long as he wasn't noticeable, it was just a matter of time before some animal came too close. And when it did, his huge jaws would instantly slam shut. Then he'd swim out into deeper water and roll over and over to be sure his meal was dead.

The alligator hoped something showed up soon. He was getting a bit cold from being in the water so much. How he longed to lie on the riverbank and bask in the sun! But there'd be time enough for that once his belly was full. Right now, he had to get rid of this hunger.

Find in the passage the answers to these questions.

Who or What?: _____

Did What?: _____

When?: _____all day long_____

Where?: _____

Why?: _____

How?: _____

Passage 5

Escaped pets can be dangerous to the environment. Sound silly? It's not. When any animal—whether a pet or wild—enters the habitat of other creatures, it can disrupt the balance of nature. A real life example of how this can happen occurred on an island. A pair of well-loved pet skunks escaped from their owners and couldn't be found.

The skunks lived happily on the island, eating all of the mice, moles, and birds' eggs they could find. With all of this food, the skunk population grew rapidly. Meanwhile, the number of birds, mice, and moles went down. The number of owls decreased, too, because they couldn't find enough mice and moles. Two little skunks had set in motion a drastic change in a food web that had worked for hundreds of years on the island.

Find in the passage the answers to these questions.

Who or What?: _____

Did What?: _____eating mice, moles, and birds' eggs_____

When?: _____

Where?: _____

Why?: _____

How?: _____

Passage 6

The Constitutional Convention was a meeting held in Philadelphia, Pennsylvania. It began in May of 1787 and lasted nearly four months. Each state—except for Rhode Island—sent a representative. Sometimes these men agreed and other times they disagreed. They argued and made changes. Step by step they wrote the United States Constitution. Today it is the supreme law of our land. It created the type of government we have and listed our basic rights.

Clerks used ink and feather quill pens to write the four pages of the Constitution. Then 39 men signed their names to it. This meant that they agreed with what it said. Some people believe that it is the most important document ever written. No wonder it took so long to write!

Find in the passage the answers to these questions.

Who or What?: _____ representatives from each state except Rhode Island _____

Did What?: _____

When?: _____

Where?: _____

Why?: _____

How?: _____

Passage 7

The Transcontinental Railroad allowed people to travel by train across the entire width of the U.S.A. Building it had taken years of work. Most of it had to be done by hand. The work was hard and often dangerous. Many men lost their lives blasting tunnels through mountains. Still, lots of men signed up to build the railroad.

Railroad crews started at each of America's coasts. One crew started laying tracks at the East Coast. They headed west as fast as they could. The other crew began laying tracks at the West Coast. They headed east as fast as they could. The crews met each other when the rails joined in Utah on May 10, 1869. A big celebration marked the railroad's completion.

Find the answers in the passage. Some of the questions may not be answered.

Who or What?: _____

Did What?: _____ was completed _____

When?: _____

Where?: _____

Why?: _____

How?: _____

Passage 8

Grace sank back on her heels to admire her work. Her castle had four towers joined by thick walls. She had used a stick to form windows and carve lines, giving the outer walls the appearance of rock. Several sticks pressed closely together formed an open drawbridge over a moat. She smiled in satisfaction. It really looked pretty good. It might even have been her best ever. No one walking on the beach would pass by this castle without giving it a second glance.

Find the answers in the passage. Two of the questions are not answered.

Who or What?: _____

Did What?: _____

When?: _____

Where?: _____on a beach_____

Why?: _____

How?: _____

Passage 9

One day the jealous brothers came up with a wicked plan to rid themselves of Zimbi. They said to him, "Come, let us go to the great pit to dig up some more of that metal which the white men value so much. Then we will trade it for more of their goods." Zimbi agreed, and each brother took up a shovel and started out. Once they reached the pit, each brother jumped in, and one at a time they dug up some of the earth, tossing glittering stones up to where the other waited. When Zimbi jumped in, however, a rain of dirt fell upon him. Each of his brothers shoveled soil into the pit as fast as possible. When Zimbi tried to climb out, one of them swung his shovel at him. Startled, Zimbi fell backwards and hit his head. As he lay unconscious, they quickly covered his body with dirt, burying him alive. Then they hurried back home to report that Zimbi was dead.

They told their parents that Zimbi had fallen into the pit and hit his head. Then one of the pit's walls had collapsed, smothering him alive. Although they had tried to rescue him, they found he was no longer breathing. The father, beside himself with grief, ordered his most trusted servants to bring his beloved son's body to him.

Find the answers in the passage. One of the questions is not answered.

Who or What?: _____Zimbi's brothers_____

Did What?: _____

When?: _____

Where?: _____

Why?: _____

How?: _____

Knowing these facts will help you locate topic sentences:

☞ **A topic sentence states the main idea of a paragraph.**

☞ **Topic sentences are often used in nonfiction text.**

☞ **Usually topic sentences come at the start of a paragraph and are followed by details.**

☞ **Sometimes topic sentences fall in the middle of a paragraph. They are surrounded on both sides by details.**

☞ **Occasionally, topic sentences come at the end of a paragraph. They sum up the details that have come before.**

Passage 1

She stared in shock at the tiny cottage. Cracked and peeling paint clung to the siding. Several roof shingles had fallen, revealing the wood beneath. Beside its grime-coated windows, broken shutters hung at crazy angles. Weeds pressed so close and high around the structure that it seemed trapped. This wasn't the vacation cabin she had expected!

Check one of the boxes to complete this sentence:

The topic sentence in this paragraph comes at the ❑ beginning ❑ middle ❑ end.

What is the topic sentence?

ⓐ Weeds pressed so close and high around the structure that it seemed trapped.

ⓑ This wasn't the vacation cabin she had expected!

ⓒ She stared in shock at the tiny cottage.

ⓓ Beside its grime-coated windows, broken shutters hung at crazy angles.

Passage 2

When oxygen comes in contact with most metals, they rust. Aluminum does not rust. It reacts with oxygen in a different way. It forms a tough surface film that stops rust. This is why people use aluminum to make cars and airplanes. It's also used as a building material. Your home may have aluminum siding. However, aluminum does not have the strength of steel. When weight must be supported, even rusty steel works better than aluminum.

Check one of the boxes to complete this sentence:

The topic sentence in this paragraph comes at the ❑ beginning ❑ middle ❑ end.

What is the topic sentence?

ⓐ When weight must be supported, even rusty steel is better than aluminum.

ⓑ Your home may have aluminum siding.

ⓒ Aluminum is often used to make cars and airplanes.

ⓓ Aluminum does not rust.

Locating Topic Sentences

Passage 3

The Black Plague killed about one-third of Europe's whole population in just four years. This sickness wiped out 50,000 people in Paris alone! The Plague swept through Europe from 1347–1351. Back then people knew almost nothing about germs or sanitary conditions. They had no idea how the disease spread. Rats ran everywhere. Fleas lived on the rats. These fleas carried the deadly Black Plague germ. Just before the Plague broke out, people had killed off a great many cats. Up until then the cats had kept the rat population in check. With fewer cats, there were more rats than ever before. And every rat harbored the plague-infested fleas in its fur. If only there had been more cats, the Black Plague would not have been as bad.

Check one of the boxes to complete this sentence:

The topic sentence in this paragraph comes at the ❏ beginning ❏ middle ❏ end.

What is the topic sentence?

ⓐ The Black Plague killed about one-third of Europe's whole population in just four years.

ⓑ The Plague swept through Europe from 1347-1351.

ⓒ If only there had been more cats, the Black Plague would not have been so bad.

ⓓ Every rat harbored the plague-infested fleas in its fur.

Passage 4

Gina followed Amy into the room. She hoped she hid her shock at how little furniture it held. Except for a well-worn couch, a few beanbag cushions, and a wood stove to provide heat during cold weather, the room was nearly empty. A stack of cardboard boxes formed makeshift shelves. Then Gina noticed the dainty painted stenciling on the otherwise bare walls. Simple, homemade curtains hung at the windows. She smiled. Although the Pages had little money, they did what they could to make their home attractive.

Check one of the boxes to complete this sentence:

The topic sentence in this paragraph comes at the ❏ beginning ❏ middle ❏ end.

What is the topic sentence?

ⓐ Although the Pages had little money, they did what they could to make their home attractive.

ⓑ Except for a well-worn couch, a few beanbag cushions, and a wood stove to provide heat during cold weather, the room was nearly empty.

ⓒ She hoped she hid her shock at how little furniture it contained.

ⓓ Gina followed Amy into the room.

Passage 5

Several problems in the American economy caused the Great Depression. Some people put their money into stocks. When the stock market crashed, lots of businesses and investors went bankrupt. Other people had put their money into banks. They thought it was a safe way to keep cash. Unfortunately, many of the banks made bad loans. When the people couldn't pay back the money they had borrowed, the banks ran out of money. They closed down. This meant that many people lost their life savings. Unemployment soared as one out of every three workers lost his job.

Check one of the boxes to complete this sentence:

The topic sentence in this paragraph comes at the ❑ beginning ❑ middle ❑ end.

What is the topic sentence?

ⓐ Several problems in the American economy caused the Great Depression.

ⓑ Unemployment soared as one out of every three workers lost his job.

ⓒ When the stock market crashed, lots of businesses and investors went bankrupt.

ⓓ Many people lost their life savings.

Passage 6

When you see the black and white and bushy tail of a skunk, you probably know to stay back. Skunks have a bad reputation for spraying awful-smelling oil at people and animals that get too close. Yet skunks don't like their own odor. Skunks spray only as a last resort. In fact, on a windy day, they often choose to run away rather than spray an enemy. They don't want the stinky oil to blow onto their own fur.

Skunks try several things before they spray. As a coyote, wolf, or cat moves toward it, the skunk arches its back and raises its tail in the air in order to look big and scary. Next, the skunk hisses, grinds its teeth, and stamps its feet. If none of those tactics work, the skunk may do a handstand. It may even walk on its hands. The skunk hopes that this will make the predator see it as large and threatening. However, sometimes people find this behavior so interesting that they move closer to get a better look or a photograph. Then the frustrated skunk sprays, hitting targets up to 16 feet (5 m) away.

Check one of the boxes to complete this sentence:

The topic sentence in this paragraph comes at the ❑ beginning ❑ middle ❑ end.

What is the topic sentence?

ⓐ Skunks have a bad reputation for spraying awful-smelling oil at people and animals that get too close.

ⓑ Skunks don't want the stinky oil to blow onto their own fur.

ⓒ When you see the black and white and bushy tail of a skunk, you probably know to stay back.

ⓓ Skunks spray only as a last resort.

Passage 7

The people of Ancient Greece had many accomplishments. They wrote history, poetry, and literature. They built outdoor theaters and put on plays. Wise men spent time thinking and talking about truth and wisdom. People studied math and medicine. Their civilization was so advanced that they had the world's first democracy. The Greeks also made beautiful statues and built stone buildings with fancy columns. Some of these are still standing today.

Check one of the boxes to complete this sentence:

The topic sentence in this paragraph comes at the ❏ beginning ❏ middle ❏ end.

What is the topic sentence?

ⓐ The Greeks also made beautiful statues and built stone buildings with fancy columns.

ⓑ Their civilization was so advanced that they had the world's first democracy.

ⓒ Wise men spent time thinking and talking about truth and wisdom.

ⓓ The people of Ancient Greece had many accomplishments.

Passage 8

At last they spied the frame of a steel roller coaster in the distance. The children pressed their noses to the car's windows. As more of the park came into view, they eagerly pointed out the water slides and other rides. Everybody started talking at once. Everyone wanted to go on a different ride first. The whole family was excited about spending the day at Endless Fun Park.

Check one of the boxes to complete this sentence:

The topic sentence in this paragraph comes at the ❏ beginning ❏ middle ❏ end.

What is the topic sentence?

ⓐ Everyone wanted to go on a different ride first.

ⓑ At last they spied the frame of a roller coaster in the distance.

ⓒ The whole family was excited about spending the day at Endless Fun Park.

ⓓ Everybody started talking at once.

Passage 9

Many people think that red-hot lava and poisonous gases are the only dangers of volcanoes. But volcanoes can also cause deadly mudflows. In November, 1985, a volcano erupted in Colombia. The ice covering the mountain quickly melted. It mixed with ash and soil to form mud. The mud raced down the side of the mountain toward a town 40 miles away. The town leaders warned their people to escape. They told them to climb a nearby hill for safety. But many of the people said that they weren't afraid of some mud. People did not want to leave their homes and go out into the rain. Few acted on the warning.

While they slept, the mudflow gushed into town. It buried everything and everyone under a deep layer of mud. Over 25,000 people died that night because they didn't realize the fatal danger of a mudflow.

Check one of the boxes to complete this sentence:

The topic sentence in this paragraph comes at the ❑ beginning ❑ middle ❑ end.

What is the topic sentence?

ⓐ The town leaders warned their people to escape.

ⓑ Volcanoes can also cause deadly mudflows.

ⓒ In November, 1985, a volcano erupted in Colombia.

ⓓ Over 25,000 people died because they didn't realize the fatal danger of a mudflow.

Passage 10

Have you ever wondered why polar bears live where it's cold or why camels live in the desert? Did you know that a tortoise and a turtle would die if you moved them to each other's environments? All species have body features and habits that help them to survive in their specific habitat. So animals that live where it's dry will not thrive—and may even die—in a moist climate. Tortoises live in the desert. They would hate a box turtle's pond. Their bodies are not adapted for swimming or living in water. Of course, the box turtle would surely die in the desert. It needs a pond to live in. The same is true if you switched a polar bear and camel. The polar bear has such a thick layer of fat and dense fur that it must live in cold areas. Otherwise, its body would overheat. The camel is adapted to the desert and thus has no protection from the cold.

Check one of the boxes to complete this sentence:

The topic sentence in this paragraph comes at the ❑ beginning ❑ middle ❑ end.

What is the topic sentence?

ⓐ All species have body features and habits that help them to survive in their specific habitat.

ⓑ Animals that live where it's dry will not thrive—and may even die—in a moist climate.

ⓒ The box turtle would surely die in the desert.

ⓓ The camel is adapted to the desert and thus has no protection from the cold.

Passage 11

Have you ever noticed the letters "PED XING" printed on a sign or painted on a road? It appears in places where people, or pedestrians, often cross the road. PED XING stands for pedestrian crossing. It gives drivers a warning to watch for people. PED XING appears before the actual crosswalk to give drivers time to look around. Of course, people usually cross streets at the corner between the painted lines of a crosswalk. But sometimes a crosswalk is needed far from a street corner, such as when a golf course is on both sides of a road. That's when PED XING can help keep people safe.

Check one of the boxes to complete this sentence:

The topic sentence in this paragraph comes at the ❑ beginning ❑ middle ❑ end.

What is the topic sentence?

(a) PED XING appears before the actual crosswalk to give drivers time to look around.

(b) Sometimes a crosswalk is needed far from a street corner, such as when a golf course is on both sides of a road.

(c) People usually cross streets at the corner between the painted lines of a crosswalk.

(d) That's when PED XING can help keep people safe.

Passage 12

Polar bears wander the icy, cold tundra around Hudson Bay, Siberia, and Greenland. Temperatures rarely rise above the freezing mark. For days at a time, the temperature never gets above -30°F (-34°C). Ice fills the Arctic Ocean during winter, virtually joining the continents. The bears are well suited to these harsh conditions. Their thick fur coat and a dense layer of fat just below their skin protect them from the extreme cold. These features allow them to swim 20 miles (32 km) through icy water and get out wet in bitter wind. Their sharp claws grip the ice, and thick fur on their footpads prevents slipping and sliding. They move across the ice at the top of the world with grace and confidence. Polar bears thrive where few other creatures would even survive.

Check one of the boxes to complete this sentence:

The topic sentence in this paragraph comes at the ❑ beginning ❑ middle ❑ end.

What is the topic sentence?

(a) Ice fills the Arctic Ocean during winter, virtually joining the continents.

(b) Polar bears thrive where few other creatures would even survive.

(c) Polar bears wander the icy cold tundra around Hudson Bay, Siberia, and Greenland.

(d) They move across the ice at the top of the world with grace and confidence.

Passage 13

Zoe looked at the lot and sighed. Maybe she should have chosen a different community service project. She would have to do hours and hours of hard work to do this alone. It certainly wasn't going to be easy cleaning up this mess. Tin cans, bottles, old newspapers, and empty milk jugs lay tangled in the thistles and weeds. Old car tires, a pile of broken bricks, and a TV set with a smashed screen were the most obvious pieces of junk. Zoe shook her head and wondered why people viewed vacant lots as garbage dumps.

Check one of the boxes to complete this sentence:

The topic sentence in this paragraph comes at the ❑ beginning ❑ middle ❑ end.

What is the topic sentence?

ⓐ It certainly wasn't going to be easy cleaning up this mess.

ⓑ Tin cans, bottles, old newspapers, and empty milk jugs lay tangled in the thistles and weeds.

ⓒ Zoe looked at the lot and sighed.

ⓓ Maybe she should have chosen a different community service project.

Passage 14

Today, America and Mexico are friends, but it wasn't always that way. President James Polk wanted to enlarge the nation. He wanted the U.S. to reach all the way from the Atlantic Ocean to the Pacific Ocean. He offered to buy from Mexico the area that is today called the American Southwest. Mexico would not sell. So from 1846 to 1848, Mexico and America fought a war. Each country wanted to own that land. When the war ended, the Rio Grande River formed the new border. America is on the north side of the river. Mexico is on the south side. Since that war, the borders have stayed the same.

Check one of the boxes to complete this sentence:

The topic sentence in this paragraph comes at the ❑ beginning ❑ middle ❑ end.

What is the topic sentence?

ⓐ So from 1846 to 1848, Mexico and America fought a war.

ⓑ When the war ended, the Rio Grande River formed the new border.

ⓒ Today, America and Mexico are friends, but it wasn't always that way.

ⓓ President James Polk wanted to enlarge the nation.

The main idea is not always stated in a paragraph or passage. This is especially true in fiction. Figure out an unstated main idea by making a "movie in your mind." Forming pictures as you read gives you a sense of the key idea.

When the main idea is not directly stated in nonfiction, gather details by keeping questions in mind (see page 15). Use the answers to piece together the main idea.

Passage 1

Bitterly cold wind and flakes of snow drifted through the cracks in the walls. The girls huddled close together in a corner of the cold barn. They had pulled bunches of loose straw around themselves to form a makeshift blanket. They listened to the blizzard raging outside. Their parents would be so worried about them! Thank goodness they'd found this shelter. Being outdoors during a blizzard was often deadly. Now they faced the problem of staying warm enough to survive until the storm ended.

What is the main idea?

ⓐ There's a blizzard raging outside a barn.

ⓑ The girls are safe now that they've found shelter.

ⓒ The girls surrounded themselves with straw.

ⓓ The girls are in a barn, hoping to live through a blizzard.

Passage 2

Think about sinking your teeth into a delicious slice of watermelon on a summer day. What makes the watermelon taste so good? Well, this juicy fruit is about 93 percent water. This makes it almost as refreshing as a glass of water on a hot, sunny day. And it provides you with vitamins A and C, as well as potassium. Since watermelons grow on vines and must be replanted each year, scientists call them vegetables. Don't you wish that all vegetables tasted so good?

What is the main idea?

ⓐ Since watermelons grow on vines and must be replanted each year, scientists call them vegetables.

ⓑ Watermelon not only tastes good, it's good for you.

ⓒ A slice of watermelon is nearly as refreshing as a glass of water on a hot summer day.

ⓓ Watermelons are about 93 percent water.

Passage 3

The rabbit zigzagged through the field, springing off rocks and diving under bushes. Behind it came the sounds of the fox crashing through the underbrush. The rabbit dared not pause to see if the fox was getting closer. Better to keep eyes to the ground in search of a burrow—no matter whose it was! The rabbit would prefer to face an outraged groundhog than the sharp claws and teeth of the fox.

What is the main idea?

ⓐ A rabbit is trying to escape from a hungry fox.

ⓑ A fox is getting tangled up in underbrush.

ⓒ The rabbit wants to meet a groundhog in its burrow.

ⓓ A rabbit is springing off of rocks and diving under bushes in a field.

Passage 4

A virus is not alive. Yet if it gets into your body, it can take over your cells and make you very sick. The most common viruses are colds and the flu. With most sicknesses, you will get better within two weeks. However, some viruses—like AIDS—may kill you.

Many deadly viruses are no longer a problem. But this is not due to antibiotics. Antibiotics fight only bacteria. Instead, we have vaccines (shots) to keep us from getting viruses. Each vaccine can only protect you from a certain virus. It cannot fight bacteria. Bacteria are living things that change over time.

What is the main idea?

ⓐ Some viruses can kill you.

ⓑ Antibiotics fight bacteria.

ⓒ Viruses can make you ill.

ⓓ A virus is not a living thing.

Passage 5

In the meantime the empress and her son eagerly awaited the bride's arrival. Weeks passed, and then a month passed. They began to fear that a tragedy had befallen the entire bridal party. At last the men returned. They told how they had been lured deep into the forest by the wood fairies and had left the princess unguarded and alone. When they finally came to their senses and returned for her, she was gone. They had spent weeks searching everywhere, but she had simply vanished. The queen flew into a rage and ordered all the men thrown into the dungeon. Then she and the prince came up with a plan to find his bride. They decided that the bridegroom must lead a group of the nation's most trusted hunters to search for the missing princess.

What is the main idea?

(a) The men lost the bride, so now the future emperor must look for her.

(b) The men were lured away from the bride by wood fairies.

(c) The bride magically vanished into thin air.

(d) The queen threw some foolish men into her dungeon.

Passage 6

Did you know that dead leaves, grass clippings, and apple peels are valuable natural resources? Instead of throwing these things in the trash, you can put them to good use. You can create a compost pile. Composting recycles plant materials. It breaks them down into minerals and returns them to the soil.  Adding composted soil to a garden helps to grow stronger, healthier plants. And composting keeps plant waste out of trash dumps. Some cities compost on a large scale in order to stop organic material from taking up space in landfills.

What is the main idea?

(a) Dead leaves, grass clipping, and apple peels are valuable natural resources.

(b) Composted soil helps gardens to grow.

(c) Some cities compost on a large scale to reduce the trash in landfills.

(d) Composting is a natural recycling method.

Passage 7

Suburbs are the areas surrounding a city. Most suburbs have large neighborhoods called housing developments. Some of the streets in these housing developments may end in a circle called a cul-de-sac. Usually there are houses all around the circle. Since there's only one way in and out of the circle, there is very little traffic. Some people think this makes a cul-de-sac an ideal place to live.

What is the main idea?

(a) You'll never find a cul-de-sac inside a city.

(b) Suburbs have housing developments which may contain cul-de-sacs.

(c) Suburbs are the areas surrounding a city.

(d) A cul-de-sac is the ideal place to live.

Passage 8

When Nyla finally reached her village, her mother and father were glad to see her. But their joy did not last when they heard how the bridegroom's tribe had treated their beloved daughter. They knew that their daughter wasn't an evil enchantress, but they had no way to prove it. They also had no desire to see their daughter return to the tribe that had accused her. Instead they returned the bridal gift of 100 horses to the bridegroom's father. Nyla took her place in her father's home once more.

Although she immediately started doing her beautiful needlework as well as ever, her heart was broken because she had lost her love. She kept busy to avoid the pain of thinking of all that had happened. No men came to ask for her hand in marriage, for far and wide people had heard the tale of the bewitched turtle. Even many of her own people who had known her since birth looked at her with fear. Time passed. It began to look as if Nyla would never be a bride.

What is the main idea?

(a) Nyla's parents are upset when they have to return the 100 horses the bridegroom had paid for her.

(b) Unfairly accused of being an enchantress, Nyla returns home to find others afraid of her.

(c) Nobody wants to marry Nyla.

(d) Nyla is not really an enchantress.

Passage 9

The young detectives couldn't hide how upset they felt at the news. If Bart Stillwell dies without confessing or telling anyone where he hid the jewels, this mystery may never be solved. Worse yet, Mrs. Goz's name may never be cleared. She may have to spend the rest of her life under a cloud of suspicion. She may never find another job. After all, who would hire a home health aide who'd been accused of stealing jewelry from her employer?

What is the main idea?

ⓐ The detectives think that Mrs. Goz may suffer if Bart Stillwell dies.

ⓑ Mrs. Goz lives under a cloud of suspicion.

ⓒ The detectives want Bart Stillwell to die.

ⓓ Mrs. Goz is terrified that Bart Stillwell may die.

Passage 10

Throughout the Empire the human race was viewed as a failure. Humans were seen as small, weak, and not very intelligent. Yet today the fate of the entire Empire lay in the hands of a human being. Everything depended upon Stan. He must sneak his small spaceship through the line of enemy defense to reach the great Anton starship. Stan carried the crystal disc aboard his craft. It alone held the secret that could defeat the Gordoks. If for any reason he failed to get the disc to the starship, nothing could stop their evil plans to take control of the entire galaxy.

What is the main idea?

ⓐ The Gordoks want to make sure that Stan reaches the Anton starship safely.

ⓑ Stan is a foolish human being, but he has an important job to do every day.

ⓒ Stan can save the Empire from the Gordoks if he gets a crystal disc to the Anton starship.

ⓓ The crystal disc will stop the Gordoks' plan to take control of the galaxy.

Passage 11

The cook carefully measured the ingredients for a chocolate cake. This was the biggest feast the queen had ordered in years. It probably meant that she'd been successful in getting King Alu to come. The cook frowned as he realized that he could afford to make no errors. His cooking must be its finest for such an important visitor.

What is the main idea?

ⓐ The cook is busy preparing a fabulous meal for an important guest.

ⓑ The queen finally convinced King Alu to come for a visit.

ⓒ The cook is making a chocolate cake because that's King Alu's favorite dessert.

ⓓ The cook doesn't enjoy his job.

Passage 12

Years ago, 100,000 grizzly bears lived in the United States. Now there are only about 1,000 (not including those that live in Alaska). In 1975 a law was passed to keep people from hunting the bears or destroying their homes. As a result, today there are many more bears than in 1975. Almost all of them live in Yellowstone National Park.

Sometimes the bears leave the park and kill cows or sheep. Some people feel afraid. They want to be able to shoot any grizzly that leaves the park. However, others say that the bear population is already too small. They do not want the law changed.

What is the main idea?

(a) Grizzly bears like to eat cows and sheep.

(b) Some grizzly bears have left Yellowstone National Park and caused trouble.

(c) Today most grizzly bears live in Alaska.

(d) There are too many grizzly bears living inside Yellowstone National Park.

Passage 13

Sam walked for a very long time. His stomach reminded him that he hadn't eaten since dawn. Still he trudged along the forest path until at last he saw a quaint little cottage in a clearing. At the door of the cottage stood a lovely lady.

"Do come in!" she said, waving a welcoming hand toward the cottage door. She immediately set a steaming bowl of chicken noodle soup in front of him. Sam felt delighted at his stroke of good fortune. But before Sam had taken two spoonfuls of the soup, a broom flew from the corner and began beating him about the head and shoulders. As he tried to shield himself from the blows, he saw that his soup was now a slimy brew filled with toads. Terrified, he looked at the woman and found that she had turned into an ugly old witch draped in a heavy black robe.

What is the main idea?

(a) A broom attacks Sam.

(b) Sam chokes on his soup when a broom hits him.

(c) Sam's chicken noodle soup is full of toads.

(d) Sam sits down to a meal, unaware that he's in a witch's home.

Choosing the Best Title

To select a title, first decide what the main idea is. Then check your choices to see which one best fits the topic.

Passage 1

The census counts every person living in the U.S. on a certain date. The census tells where Americans live and the size of their families. It tells how many people have come from other places. It shows the number of people in each age group. The census finds out what people do for a living, how much money they earn, and how much education they have. It reports the number of births, deaths, marriages, and divorces.

The Constitution requires a census once a decade to decide how many people each state should have in the House of Representatives. The states with the biggest population send the most people to Congress. States with fewer people send less. After a census, some states may gain seats in the House of Representatives. Other states may lose seats.

What is the best title for this passage?
ⓐ A Constitutional Requirement
ⓑ Finding Out About Americans' Income
ⓒ U.S. Census Provides Essential Data
ⓓ American Citizens Respond to U.S. Census

Passage 2

Flames threw strange, dancing shadows on their tent. The hearty smell of smoke rose from the crackling campfire. Karlene's dad emerged from the darkness just beyond the circle of firelight, carrying two long twigs. He held their tips to the flames to clean the ends of the branches. Then he handed one to Karlene, along with a marshmallow. She pressed it onto the blackened twig tip and held the fluffy white cube over some embers at the edge of the fire. When it turned golden brown, she popped it into her mouth. Looking at her father across the flickering flames, she smiled. Time alone with her dad and toasted marshmallows. This must be paradise.

What is the best title for this passage?
ⓐ A Dangerous Camping Trip
ⓑ Karlene's Campfire
ⓒ Enjoying Nature
ⓓ Toasting Marshmallows

Passage 3

The Pilgrims arrived in Plymouth, Massachusetts in December 1620. During that winter many of them died of the cold, illness, and a lack of food. Less than half of them lived until spring. That's when the Native Americans found the starving people. They showed them how to plant corn and beans. They showed them the best places to fish. The Pilgrims probably could not have survived without their help.

After their first harvest, the Pilgrims felt very grateful that they had food to make it through the next winter. So they held the first Thanksgiving in the fall of 1621. They invited the Native Americans to a meal that lasted for three whole days. They gave thanks to God and looked forward to their future in the New World.

What is the best title for this passage?

Ⓐ The Pilgrims' First Winter

Ⓑ The First Thanksgiving

Ⓒ Thanking the Native Americans

Ⓓ A Massachusetts Celebration

Passage 4

The lions readily accepted the kitty cat as a member of their pride (family). They were even glad to share their food with her. But the biggest lion often nearly stepped on her. He meant no harm, but he was clumsy. Once he accidentally stomped right on Mandy's tender tail. Her poor tail throbbed with pain for three days.

To make matters worse, all of the lions snored loudly each night, keeping Mandy awake and making her very nervous. Each time a zoo worker came around, she had to hide so that she wouldn't be noticed and thrown out. Mandy felt a twinge of loneliness for Suzy. Maybe this wasn't where she belonged after all.

What is the best title for this passage?

Ⓐ When Mandy Lived with Lions

Ⓑ Lions Snore

Ⓒ Mandy Loves Lions

Ⓓ Mandy Gets Hurt

Passage 5

A storm surge is not a tidal wave. It comes ashore with a hurricane. During a hurricane, strong winds whip the ocean into huge, towering waves. The first big waves reach land when the center of the storm is still 100 miles out to sea. But when the storm itself hits the shore, the bulge of water directly under the storm's eye smashes into the coast. It can gush up to a mile inland, flooding homes, stores, and streets. When the water flows back to the ocean, it drags things such as cars and houses out to sea. Fortunately storm surges can be predicted, so people can leave the area before one strikes.

What is the best title for this passage?
- (a) Hurricanes
- (b) Terrifying Tidal Waves
- (c) Tornadoes Cause Storm Surges
- (d) The Danger of Storm Surges

Passage 6

At night it was pitch black in his corner of the alley, but he dared not leave his spot. Another beggar would quickly take his space, for at least it was out of the bitter cold wind. The beggar hated the darkness, but he had no money. He couldn't even buy a candle. Then he remembered the matchbox he had found on the road and how the strange old woman had told him it had great value. He fumbled in his pocket and removed the matchbox. While he could see no great value in the object, at least he could light one of its matches and thereby erase this wretched darkness for a few moments. He struck the match on the end of the box. A tiny flame erupted from its end. Much to his surprise, a gigantic hound also appeared and said, "What do you wish, master?"

The beggar's mouth dropped open and he couldn't speak for a full minute. When he found his voice, he said, "Fetch me some money!"

The hound disappeared as quickly as he'd appeared. Within a quarter of an hour he returned, lugging a huge sack filled with gold coins.

What is the best title for this passage?
- (a) The Huge Hound
- (b) Striking Matches
- (c) The Amazing Matchbox
- (d) On a Cold, Dark Night

Passage 7

Her father's face darkened in a frown when he saw Kleota's companion. The Oracle was proud of the fact that he had never had anything to do with Earthlings. He saw them as ignorant and beneath his race. Thus, he did not contain his rage when his daughter stated her plans to marry the Earthling.

In spite of his fury, Kleota refused to back down. She told her parents of Ethan's power and wisdom, but to no avail. Her mother, afraid of displeasing her husband, did not take the young lovers' side.

Nothing Kleota said made any impression on the Oracle. He said that no Kryptonite had ever married an Earthling, and his daughter would not be the first to do so. When her father demanded he be returned to Earth immediately, Kleota threw her arms around Ethan and refused to let go. Finally the Oracle allowed the Earthling to stay, but it was only to give him time to come up with a plan to get rid of the Earthling.

What is the best title for this passage?

(a) Kleota Faces the Oracle's Fury

(b) Ethan's Sweetheart

(c) Kleota Marries Ethan

(d) The Oracle's Decision

Passage 8

The Chinese made the first magnetic compass. They developed fishing reels, wheelbarrows, matches, and umbrellas. Paper and gunpowder are also their inventions. They had paper as early as 200 A.D. They began using paper money 700 years later, about the same time that they invented gunpowder. Ancient China had all of these things hundreds of years before anyone else.

The rest of the world did not know about these things for a long time. Few people traveled to or from China. The highest mountain range in the world separated China from the rest of the continent.

What is the best title for this passage?

(a) Ancient Chinese Inventors

(b) Ancient Chinese Inventions

(c) Ancient Chinese Used Paper Money

(d) Europe Discovers Chinese Inventions

Passage 9

Stomach acid spun us around and around until we all felt at least a little bit dizzy. Then the stomach's muscles squeezed us, pushing us into the small intestine. The headlights on our ship shone on the pink walls of the small intestine. Our ship zipped along the intestine. I felt like I was going down a long, winding road. Floating outside our craft's windows were little bits of food, pieces so tiny that you would normally need a microscope to detect them. Of course, since we weren't much bigger than they were, we could easily see them. More juices spilled over us. Since our ship couldn't be digested, it got directed into the large intestine.

What is the best title for this passage?

(a) A New Amusement Ride

(b) A Scary Trip

(c) A Choppy Ride

(d) Voyage Through the Intestines

Passage 10

Many blind people have trained guide dogs to help them get around. Yet nobody set out to train guide dogs; it happened by accident! Near the end of World War I, a German doctor went for a walk outside a hospital. He had his dog and a blind patient with him. Someone called the doctor back inside. When he returned, he found that his dog had led the blind man all the way across the hospital grounds. This made the doctor wonder if a dog could be trained to lead a blind person. He started working with his dog, and with other dogs as well. His results were a success. In 1929 an American reporter wrote about the German's guide dog program. This led to the creation of the first American guide dog school.

Guide dogs learn the meaning of voice commands and hand gestures. They also learn when to disobey in order to protect their owners. For example, if a guide dog is told to lead the person across a street, but sees a speeding truck, it will keep the person from stepping into the road. A guide dog must also learn to make decisions—such as what to do when the sidewalk is blocked.

What is the best title for this passage?

(a) Being Blind

(b) First American Guide Dog School

(c) Guide Dogs Help the Blind

(d) A Startling Discovery

Passage 11

A quarry must be dug in an area with the right kind of rock or sand. Most often the place chosen is in a rural area. After all, it would be difficult to dig a massive hole in the middle of a city! And that's just what a quarry is: a large pit. Big digging machines remove rock or sand from the earth. Dynamite can also blast the rocks loose. In some quarries chunks of rock get crushed into gravel. Dump trucks move the gravel to where it's needed for roads, sidewalks, and driveways.

In other quarries workers remove marble or granite in huge sheets. They must move slowly and carefully to keep these valuable rocks from splitting. After cutting and polishing, they make beautiful floors, desktops, and headstones.

It can take dozens of years to remove all of the material from a quarry, but eventually it does run out. Often rainwater and groundwater fill the pit left behind, forming a deep lake. Sometimes an abandoned quarry can be lined with plastic and used as a landfill for garbage.

What is the best title for this passage?
(a) Finding Marble
(b) Digging a Big Hole
(c) Using Granite
(d) Quarries

Passage 12

The Statue of Liberty is the most recognized statue in the world. As an American symbol, not everyone realizes that it was actually made in France. The French people wanted to give Miss Liberty to America as a 100th birthday gift. Yet it was too big to send all in one piece. So they took it apart and carefully packed it in 214 boxes. Then they loaded the boxes onto a ship. During the trip, the ship almost sank in an ocean storm. Fortunately the Statue arrived in the U.S.A. after several weeks at sea.

Once it got here, the Statue needed a base, but there was no money to build one. So a New York newspaper offered to print the name of every person who gave money to build the base. People sent money until enough had been raised. Finally, Miss Liberty was pieced back together and put in place. She stands proudly on Liberty Island in New York City.

What is the best title for this passage?
(a) Raising Money for Miss Liberty
(b) The Story of Miss Liberty
(c) Building a Base for the Statue of Liberty
(d) The Statue with the Flaming Torch

In order to summarize the main idea, follow these steps:

    Step 1: Look for the important words in the passage.

    Step 2: Identify how the important words relate to each other.

    Step 3: Based on Steps 1 & 2, write a sentence about the main idea.

Passage 1

The fire's terrifying roar grew louder. It sounded like a huge predator seeking to devour everything in its path. Mingled with the roar was the crack and crash of huge trees falling into the blaze. The thick black smoke made it difficult to breathe. The animals' pace slowed. They just couldn't get enough oxygen to keep running. Gasping and choking, the forest creatures kept moving steadily away from the intense heat of the advancing flames.

Follow these three steps to summarize the main idea in the passage above.

    Step 1: Underline the important words in the passage above.

    Step 2: What do these important words have in common? _____

    Step 3: Write a sentence stating the main idea: _____

_____

Passage 2

For years people tried to reach the summit of Mt. Everest. George Mallory almost made it in 1924 but died after a fall near the mountain's top. In 1953 Edmund Hillary and Tenzing Norgay reached the top. Since then hundreds of people have successfully made the climb.

Why do mountain climbers flock to Mt. Everest? What's so special about it? It's the tallest mountain in the world. Towering above the Himalayan range, it stands over 29,000 feet (8,850 m) high. Mt. Everest reaches high into the Earth's atmosphere. The air at its top is so thin that it has little oxygen, so it's hard to breathe. Nearly every climber needs bottled oxygen to reach the top.

Follow these three steps to summarize the main idea in the passage above.

    Step 1: Underline the important words in the passage above.

    Step 2: What do these important words have in common? _____

    Step 3: Write a sentence stating the main idea: _____

_____

Passage 3

Tom threw open the door and flung up his arm to shield his eyes from the brilliant light. Quartac had left through the time portal. He'd kill President Roosevelt and change the course of history! Tom knew he must follow him, despite the overwhelming nausea that always accompanied his time travels.

Tom's palms sweated heavily, and his face felt flushed. He had to run across the room, trusting that the time portal would open at the exact moment before he slammed into the wall. No matter how many times he did this, he always felt afraid.

Follow these three steps to summarize the main idea in the passage above.

   Step 1: Underline the important words in the passage above.

   Step 2: What do these important words have in common? _____

   Step 3: Write a sentence stating the main idea: _____

_____

Passage 4

Monarch butterflies are bright orange with black markings. Just like birds, they migrate every year. Thousands of people watch for them and record when and where they see them. The butterflies go south beginning in August. They leave Canada and the northern states of the U.S.A., flying up to 2,000 miles with their strong wings. The monarchs sleep through the winter in Mexico or California. In early spring they awaken and fly home to lay their eggs. After they lay the eggs, they die. But soon a new group of monarch butterflies will migrate and start the cycle over again.

Follow these three steps to summarize the main idea in the passage above.

   Step 1: Underline the important words in the passage above.

   Step 2: What do these important words have in common? _____

   Step 3: Write a sentence stating the main idea: _____

_____

Passage 5

He stood, breathing heavily, looking at the monster he'd just killed. His jaw dropped open, and he stared in amazement as a stream of men, women, children, goats, and cows spilled from the monster's gapping mouth. Since the greedy monster had eaten heartily during its life, hundreds of people and creatures emerged. There were more than enough people and animals to create a new kingdom. Each one approached Aryl and fell at his feet in gratitude, since he had slain the beast that held them captive. The people so admired Aryl that they begged him to rule their new nation.

"Thank you," he said, "but to tell you the truth, I couldn't have done it without these three little pebbles." As he spoke, he held up the little pouch containing the talking stones. Suddenly the pouch fell to the ground, and the stones leaped out of it. Then the pebbles all cracked and from them stepped three beautiful princesses. The tallest one took Aryl's hand.

Her smile was dazzling. "Because you have ended the curse that kept us trapped as pebbles, our father will give you whichever one of us you choose as your wife."

Write a sentence stating the main idea:

_____

_____

Passage 6

Susan B. Anthony was an important American. All of her life she worked for women's rights. In 1850 she teamed up with Elizabeth Cady Stanton. The two women promoted their cause through peaceful meetings and speeches. They had printed pamphlets and handed them out. They stressed that women needed to get good educations, have jobs, and own property. After a while they decided to put all of their efforts into getting women the right to vote. They felt that if women could vote, all of their other rights would follow.

In 1920 the 19th Amendment gave women the right to vote. Since she had died in 1906, Anthony did not live long enough to see the fruits of her labor. Still, people call it the Susan B. Anthony Amendment in honor of her efforts.

Write a sentence stating the main idea:

_____

_____

Passage 7

Not Brussels sprouts again! Jason hated them the most of all the vegetables his father served. He smiled innocently as his father dished them onto his plate, but his mind was at work thinking of a plan to get them off his plate and onto the floor. Then Patches would clean them up. That dog would eat anything that came off the table, convinced that human food was always more delicious than his own.

Write a sentence stating the main idea:

_____

_____

Passage 8

What do apples, tomatoes, peaches, pumpkins, and plums have in common? Yes, they are all fruits since they have seeds enclosed in fleshy bodies. And of course the fleshy part is meant to nourish the seeds. Besides these obvious similarities, they all have a special quality. They give off ethylene gas. This colorless, odorless gas makes fruit ripen. If you put a piece of fruit into a paper bag, it will ripen quickly. The ethylene gas stays trapped inside the bag, acting upon the fruit.

Write a sentence stating the main idea:

_____

_____

Passage 9

As we pulled into the dirt drive of the chinchilla ranch, my heart pounded. I really hoped that I would find the perfect pet. My mother had wanted a chinchilla for three months. She had promised that I could get one, too. Mom thought that if we got brothers, they'd be buddies who could live together in the same cage.

Now my whole family had driven for four hours to reach the farm, and our van had never seemed smaller. Although my two little brothers had been glued to their Gameboxes, they hadn't left me alone for more than three minutes at a time. I was more than a little frustrated with them as I opened the door and got out. But my mood quickly changed to excitement as soon as the breeder stepped out of the chinchilla barn to greet us.

Write a sentence stating the main idea:

_____

_____

Passage 10

Long ago, people in China wanted to protect their border. They were tired of enemies invading their country. They decided that they would build a high, thick wall. It would act like a fence to keep others out of China.

Slowly, over many years, the Great Wall of China took shape. Actually the Great Wall is made of many shorter walls joined together. It stretches for 1500 miles and averages about 25 feet in height. This makes the Great Wall the only man-made thing large enough to be seen from outer space!

Write a sentence stating the main idea:

_____

_____

Passage 11

Devin was really enjoying this nature walk. The guide seemed to know a story about every single flower, tree, and insect that they saw. Already Devin had learned that only one kind of crayfish lives on land. The chimney crayfish digs a hole in a swamp, pushing dirt up to form a "chimney." So far they'd seen three such chimneys. Devin wondered why he'd never noticed them before. He wished he could see one of the crayfish, but the guide said that they only came out at night to hunt for food.

Write a sentence stating the main idea:

_____

_____

Passage 12

So deep was King Ponu's dislike for his step daughter Princess Ria, that he spent time thinking of ways to be cruel to her. He refused to let her have any jewelry while his own daughter wore rubies and emeralds. Princess Ria wore old, stained gowns. Princess Velia's clothing was woven from the finest materials. Still the people of his kingdom admired Ria's beauty and kindness. This made the king angry.

One day after hearing another story of Ria's kindness, King Ponu's temper flared. He immediately declared that Princess Ria must wear an ogre's skin from head to toe. She must never appear in public without it. The evil king smiled. When she wore the hideous skin, the people would cease to love her. And no man would ever want to marry her.

Write a sentence stating the main idea:

_____

Passage 1

The chief called his advisors together. They came up with a clever plan by which to uncover the troll. "Dig a pit in the middle of the village and place in it a jug filled to the brim with fresh coconut milk," the chief commanded his servants. "Then every maiden of marrying age must walk all the way around the hole. No troll can resist coconut milk. We will soon discover which of these beauties is not what she seems!"

When the pit with the coconut milk was prepared, the chief watched as each young woman walked around the hole. At last it was Akiti's turn. She whined and complained that since she was to marry the chief's son, she should not be put on public display. She appealed to the chief's son himself. But the chief stood firm, and he commanded that she walk around the hole or be banished from the tribe forever.

So Akiti moved slowly to the edge of the pit. She looked away from the hole, determined not to look at the jug. The smell of the sweet liquid filled her nostrils, and they began to twitch. Akiti took a few more steps. She couldn't control herself, however, and her tail uncoiled from its hiding place under her skirt. Of its own accord, it slid into the coconut milk and sucked the jug dry in front of the astonished villagers.

1. **What is the main idea?**
   ⓐ Most of the girls are glad to walk around the pit that holds a jug full of coconut milk.
   ⓑ Akiti doesn't want to have to walk around the pit.
   ⓒ The plan works to show which maiden is actually a troll.
   ⓓ The villagers had no idea there was a troll among them.

2. **What is the topic sentence?**
   ⓐ They came up with a clever plan by which to uncover the troll.
   ⓑ No troll can resist coconut milk.
   ⓒ Akiti whined and complained that since she was to marry the chief's son, she should not be put on public display.
   ⓓ Akiti couldn't control herself, however, and her tail uncoiled from its hiding place under her skirt.

3. **What is the best title for this passage?**
   ⓐ Akiti's Complaint
   ⓑ The Chief and Akiti
   ⓒ Akiti Amazes the Villagers
   ⓓ The Troll Test

Passage 2

It took hundreds of men eight years to dig the Erie Canal by hand. New York taxpayers spent $7 million to build it. Fortunately it was money well spent. The Canal was an immediate success. When it opened in 1825, it made it possible to travel from the Hudson River to the Great Lakes entirely by water. This offered settlers a good way to get to the Midwest. Once they made it to the shores of Lake Erie, ships could carry them to Ohio, Michigan, and Minnesota.

The Canal also made farming in New York state much more profitable. To move a ton of corn or wheat from Albany to Buffalo by land cost $90–$125. To move that same amount the same distance on the Canal was a mere $5–$30. This meant that farmers could sell to markets far away and still make money.

Boats carried passengers on the Canal. Barges moved lumber, coal, grain, and other goods. Mules were hooked to the boats or barges with long, thick ropes. They walked on a path that went along the edge of the water, pulling their load down the waterway. It was exhausting work for them. So every 20 miles new mules took over.

1. **What is the main idea?**
   ⓐ The Erie Canal cost too much to build.
   ⓑ The Erie Canal made travel and movement of goods easier and cheaper.
   ⓒ Mules worked hard to pull boats and barges along the Erie Canal.
   ⓓ The Erie Canal made New York state farmers rich.

2. **What is the topic sentence?**
   ⓐ Barges carried lumber, coal, grain and other goods on the Canal.
   ⓑ New York taxpayers spent $7 million to build the Erie Canal.
   ⓒ Farmers could sell to markets far away and still make money.
   ⓓ The Canal was an immediate success.

3. **What is the best title for this passage?**
   ⓐ New Ways to Travel West
   ⓑ New York Farmers Strike it Rich
   ⓒ The Early Success of the Erie Canal
   ⓓ A Trip on the Erie Canal

Passage 3

The tribe had but one problem: a steady supply of fresh water. Everyone needed water for drinking, cooking, and cleaning. Yet the nearby stream to which the women carried their water jugs each day would sometimes abruptly stop flowing. There was neither rhyme nor reason to the dry spells. No one could predict them, for there was never any warning. Sometimes the problem lasted for days, other times for weeks. Whenever it happened, the women of the tribe had to spend most of their day walking to and from a distant pool. Nobody actually knew why this kept happening.

On the day our story begins, the women took their water jugs to fill them. When they reached the stream, however, they found it all but empty. Shallow depressions held small, muddy puddles of water, but even those would disappear under the sun's scorching rays. The women split into two groups. One group followed the stream to see if any water could be found further downstream. The other followed the stream to look for water upstream. But just as every time before, none could be found anywhere.

1. **What is the main idea?**
   ⓐ Sometimes the stream is dry, but nobody knows why.
   ⓑ A magic spell has been placed on the stream that the tribe relies upon for water.
   ⓒ The women of the tribe must carry water to the village.
   ⓓ The tribe can never get enough water from a nearby stream.

2. **What is the topic sentence?**
   ⓐ Shallow depressions held small, muddy puddles of water, but even those would disappear under the sun's scorching rays.
   ⓑ On the day our story begins, the women took their water jugs to fill them.
   ⓒ There was neither rhyme nor reason to the dry spells.
   ⓓ The tribe had but one problem: a steady supply of fresh water.

3. **What is the best title for this passage?**
   ⓐ A Tribe with a Problem
   ⓑ The Mysterious Stream
   ⓒ The Thirsty Tribe
   ⓓ Muddy Water Misery

Page 5
Passage 1: b   *Passage 2:* c

Page 6
Passage 3: d   *Passage 4:* d

Page 7
Passage 5: a   *Passage 6:* d

Page 8
Passage 7: c   *Passage 8:* a

Page 9
Passage 9: b   *Passage 10:* a

Page 10
Passage 1
Main Idea: c
Details:
- purple eyes
- horn in center of forehead
- orange skin under coarse black hair
- claws
- snarled menacingly
- sharp teeth

Page 11
Passage 2
Main Idea: a
Details:
- Liberty Bell
- American flag
- American bald eagle

Passage 3
Main Idea: d
Details:
- removed soil
- cut down trees
- built dams

Page 12
Passage 4
Main Idea: c
Details:
- cozy & welcoming
- felt safe there
- everything clean & tidy
- always delicious baking smell

Passage 5
Main Idea: d
Details:
- families lived together
- people shared crops and food from hunting
- used herbal medicines
- women assigned and removed government leaders
- formed Iroquois League

Page 13
Passage 6
Main Idea: c
Details:
- more magnificent than any other man
- strong
- long black hair
- broad chest
- muscular arms
- tall
- kind smile

Passage 7
Main Idea: a
Details:
- have same measuring system as rest of world
- easier to use with calculators
- already used in U.S. science & medicine
- cost $ to change over
- learning it could be difficult for adults
- American people have always balked at learning new system.

Page 14
Passage 8
Main Idea: b
Details:
- people built homes on Native American's land
- people made roads through Native Americans' buffalo hunting grounds
- people built towns
- Native Americans didn't believe in owning property
- fights occurred between settlers and Native Americans

Passage 9
Main Idea: a
Details:
- without plants, there'd be no life on Earth
- provide food
- give off oxygen
- provide medicines
- provide building materials
- provide materials we make into cloth

Page 15
Passage 1
Who or What: Claudia
Did What: tricked the farmer
When: at dinner
Where: in his home
Why: to get better food

How: by telling him a leprechaun magically conjured up a feast

Page 16
Passage 2
Who or What: Anasazi tribe
Did What: vanished
When: 600 years ago
Where: U.S. southwest
Why: no one knows
How: no one knows

Passage 3
Who or What: Ruth Wakefield
Did What: invented chocolate chip cookies
When: 1930
Where: at the Toll House Inn in Massachusetts
Why: she ran out of baker's chocolate
How: chocolate bits didn't melt into the cookies

Page 17
Passage 4
Who or What: alligator
Did What: waited for food
When: all day long
Where: under water
Why: to get rid of hunger
How: by staying hidden

Passage 5
Who or What: pet skunks
Did What: disrupted a food web
When: after escaping
Where: on an island
Why: took away food needed by others
How: eating mice, moles, and birds' eggs

Page 18
Passage 6
Who or What: representatives from every state except Rhode Island
Did What: went to Constitutional Convention
When: May to August 1787
Where: Philadelphia, PA
Why: to create U.S. government & citizens' basic rights
How: by debating & voting

Passage 7
Who or What: Transcontinental Railroad
Did What: was completed
When: May 10, 1869
Where: Utah
Why: to let people travel from coast to coast
How: two railroad crews laid tracks starting at each coast

Answer Key

Page 19
Passage 8
Who or What: Grace
Did What: built a sand castle
When: not given in passage
Where: on a beach
Why: not given in passage
How: using sand & sticks
Passage 9
Who or What: Zimbi's brothers
Did What: buried Zimbi alive
When: not given in passage
Where: in a pit
Why: they were jealous of him
How: they threw dirt down on him
Page 20
Passage 1
end; b
Passage 2
beginning; d
Page 21
Passage 3
end; c
Passage 4
end; a
Page 22
Passage 5
beginning; a
Passage 6
middle; d
Page 23
Passage 7
beginning; d
Passage 8
end; c
Page 24
Passage 9
beginning; b
Passage 10
middle; a
Page 25
Passage 11
end; d
Passage 12
end; b
Page 26
Passage 13
middle a
Passage 14
beginning; c
Page 27
Passage 1: d
Passage 2: b
Page 28
Passage 3: a
Passage 4: c

Page 29
Passage 5: a
Passage 6: d
Page 30
Passage 7: b
Passage 8: b
Page 31
Passage 9: a
Passage 10: c
Passage 11: a
Page 32
Passage 12: b
Passage 13: d
Page 33
Passage 1: c
Passage 2: d
Page 34
Passage 3: b
Passage 4: a
Page 35
Passage 5: d
Passage 6: c
Page 36
Passage 7: a
Passage 8: b
Page 37
Passage 9: d
Passage 10: c
Page 38
Passage 11: d
Passage 12: b
Page 39
(Be flexible on the important words identified.)
Passage 1
Words: fire, roar, blaze, smoke, animals, oxygen, choking, gasping, heat, flames
In Common: fire, breathing
Main Idea: All of the animals have difficulty breathing as they rush to escape from a raging forest fire.
Passage 2
Words: summit, mountain, climb, tallest, Mt. Everest
In Common: mountain climbing
Main Idea: Many people want to climb Mt. Everest, the tallest mountain in the world.
Page 40
Passage 3
Words: Tom, Quartac, time portal, history, travel
In Common: Tom, time portal
Main Idea: Despite Tom's fear, he must travel through a time portal to stop Quartac from changing history.

Passage 4
Words: monarch butterflies, migrate, Canada, U.S.A., Mexico, California
In common: monarch butterflies, migrate
Main Idea: The life of a monarch butterfly includes a long migration.
Page 41
Passage 5
When Aryl rescues people and animals by killing a monster, the stones that helped him turn into princesses.
Passage 6
Susan B. Anthony's efforts helped to get voting rights for American women.
Page 42
Passage 7
Jason forms a plan for getting the dog to secretly eat the Brussel sprouts he hates.
Passage 8
Ethylene gas helps different fruits to ripen.
Passage 9
After a long trip, the writer is eager to select a chinchilla to be his or her pet.
Page 43
Passage 10
The Chinese built the Great Wall of China to keep enemies from invading their nation.
Passage 11
Devin enjoys a nature walk and learns about chimney crayfish.
Passage 12
King Ponu hates Princess Ria so much that he commands that she must wear an ugly ogre skin whenever she's out in public.
Page 44
Assessment Passage 1
1. c
2. a
3. d
Page 45
Assessment Passage 2
1. b
2. d
3. c
Page 46
Assessment Passage 3
1. a
2. d
3. b

#8645 Main Idea—Grade 5 48 *©Teacher Created Resources, Inc.*